ANXIETY RELIEF WORKBOOK FOR CHRISTIAN KIDS

God's Hand Publishers

About the Author

We're glad you're here at God's Hand Publishers, a place where we produce Christian-based workbooks that help adults, kids and teenagers. At God's Hand Publishers, we have a strong conviction in the influence of faith and how it may change a person's life.

John Raymond, the founder of our organization and primary writer, is a fervent supporter of mental wellness and enlightenment. John Raymond set out on a mission to develop materials that would encourage people to view life's challenges through the prism of faith because he had a strong desire to serve God and be of service to others.

John Raymond has a background in religion and psychology. We consider it a privilege to collaborate with people, congregations, institutions of higher learning, and other groups who value spiritual development and mental health. Let's go on a spiritually-based journey of self-discovery together as we face the difficulties of life and develop into the unique people God created us to be.

Thank you for joining us on this transformative path. May God's hand guide you every step of the way, in faith and service,

God's Hand Publishers

Free Ebook for you

Scan the QR code to download

OR use the link below to download for FREE!

https://mailchi.mp/8fba038161b1/free-ebook

OTHER BOOKS FROM THIS SERIES

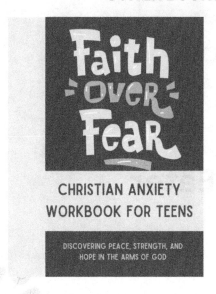

TABLE
OF CONTENTS

Introduction

Hey there, all you bright and shining stars! 🌟⭐ Life's adventure can be a wild rollercoaster, full of twists, turns, and loop-de-loops that sometimes make us go, "Whoa, slow down!" It's totally normal to feel a little jittery when faced with new challenges or big, exciting moments. But guess what? You've just picked up something amazing that's going to help you conquer those nervous butterflies and embrace each day with a mega-watt smile!

Welcome to "Rise and Shine: Anxiety Relief Workbook for Christian Kids"! 🌈 📖 Yep, you heard it right. This isn't your regular ol' workbook. Nope, it's your secret treasure map to finding calm, courage, and confidence through the awesome power of your faith. We're diving into the world of anxiety, giving it a one-two punch, and showing it who's boss - that's you!

Now, you might be wondering, "How's this gonna work?" Well, my fantastic friend, this book is packed with super fun games, thoughtful exercises, and cool stories that'll help you understand your feelings and put those worry monsters in their place. And guess what else? You're not alone on this adventure. God's right here beside you, cheering you on every step of the way.

So, get ready to explore, discover, and grow. Are you excited? We sure are! Let's laugh, learn, and leap into each page with all the enthusiasm you've got. Remember, you're never alone, and you're capable of incredible things. So what are you waiting for? Let's dive in and Rise and Shine together! ☀️🌱

PS: Don't forget to grab your crayons, a comfy pillow, and your biggest smile. Adventure awaits - turn the page and let's go! 🎉📚

CHAPTER 1

Knowing the Worry Monster

A-E OF ANXIETY

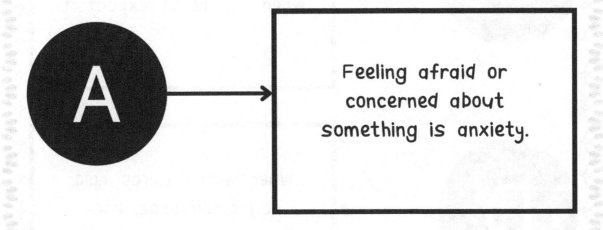

A → Feeling afraid or concerned about something is anxiety.

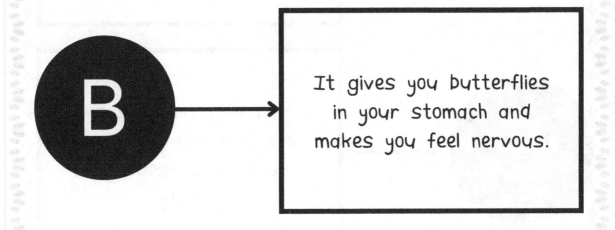

B → It gives you butterflies in your stomach and makes you feel nervous.

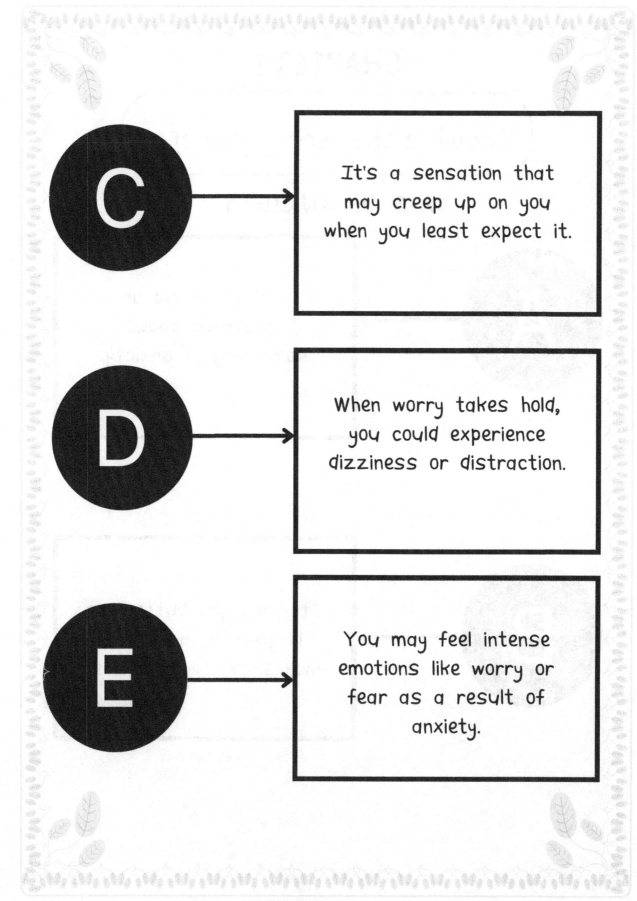

C → It's a sensation that may creep up on you when you least expect it.

D → When worry takes hold, you could experience dizziness or distraction.

E → You may feel intense emotions like worry or fear as a result of anxiety.

Amy was a bright, inquisitive young girl who adored discovering new things. Every day she looked forward to going to school, with one exception: speaking up in class. Her pulse raced every time her teacher posed a question, and every time she spoke, it was like trying to fit a jigsaw piece into an empty space.

After class one morning, Amy's friend Mia observed that she was frowning. "Are you okay, Amy? You seem worried."

Amy sighed. "I am, Mia. Whenever I have to speak in class, I get this funny feeling. It's like I can't breathe, and my thoughts run away."

Mia smiled gently. "You know what? I used to feel that way too. But then, I talked to the school counselor, Ms. Johnson. She helped me understand what it was."

Amy's eyes widened. "Really? What is it?"

"Mia leaned closer. "It's called anxiety. It's like when you're nervous or worried about something, and your body reacts in a special way."

Curiosity sparked in Amy's eyes. "Anxiety? Can you tell me more?"

Mia nodded. "Sure! Anxiety is when you feel super nervous about something, even if it's not a big deal. It's like your body's 'alarm' goes off, and you feel shaky, your heart races, and your thoughts get jumbled up."

Amy nodded slowly. "That sounds exactly like what happens to me."

Mia grinned. "That's because you're not alone, Amy. Lots of people feel anxious at times. But the good news is, you can learn to manage it!"

ACTIVITY

First task - Circle the emotions, then circle the physical reactions, and finally, the behavioral reactions you experience whenever you feel anxious.

Second task - Write out the activities or events that trigger your anxiety.

Last task - Create an "Anxiety Monster" Drawing - This activity can help you to visualize your anxiety. Draw or paint a picture of an "anxiety monster." What does it look like to you?

Circle the emotions

Worry

Nervousness

Fear

Apprehension

Unease

Panic

Restlessness

Overwhelm

Dread

anxious

Tension

Self-doubt

Insecurity

Irritability

Helplessness

Circle the physical reactions

Rapid heartbeat

Shallow or fast breathing

Trembling or shaking

Sweating

Muscle tension

Dry mouth

Nausea or upset stomach

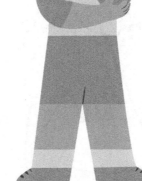

Headache

Dizziness

ANXIOUS

Clammy hands

Difficulty concentrating

Racing thoughts

Trouble sleeping

Increased sensitivity to noise or lights

Circle the behavioral reactions

fidgeting

Nail biting or other repetitive behaviors

Difficulty making decisions

Seeking reassurance from others

Seeking distractions

Procrastination

Overthinking

Trouble focusing

Increased startle response

Write out your anxiety trigger inside the circle

Below is a drawing of my own imagination of an anxiety monster, draw out yours.

Describe how your body feels whenever you feel anxious.

_____

_____

_____

What did you do to cope the last time you felt anxious?

_____

_____

_____

Say this prayer

Dear God,

With my concerns and fears, I come to you. My thoughts are often disorganized, and occasionally my heart feels heavy.

When I'm nervous, please help me maintain composure and bravery. Tell me again how strong and at peace you are with me. I have faith in your ability to relate to me on a human level and your unwavering affection for me.

Thank you for being my rock in times of trouble.

In Jesus name, Amen.

Meditate on these Bible Verses

Philippians 4:6-7 (NIV) - "Do not be anxious about anything, but in every situation, by prayer and petition, with thanksgiving, present your requests to God. And the peace of God, which transcends all understanding, will guard your hearts and your minds in Christ Jesus."

Matthew 6:34 (NIV) - "Therefore do not worry about tomorrow, for tomorrow will worry about itself. Each day has enough trouble of its own."

Isaiah 41:10 (NIV) - "So do not fear, for I am with you; do not be dismayed, for I am your God. I will strengthen you and help you; I will uphold you with my righteous right hand."

CHAPTER 2

God's Got this

JOB'S FAITH IN GOD

The life of Job is a well-known illustration of how someone who was experiencing anxiety turned to God for support.

Job had everything he could possibly want since he was wealthy and prosperous.

But one day, things started to shift. In addition to his health, Job also lost his employees, children, and animals. He had nothing left, and he was anxious and dejected.

In his hour of hardship, Job might have easily turned away from God. But he made the decision to pray to God instead. In addition to expressing his rage and dissatisfaction to God, he also demonstrated his faith in him.

Despite not understanding why he was experiencing such severe anguish, he was aware that God was in charge.

God ultimately heard Job's prayers. He did restore Job's health and prosperity, but He didn't explain why Job had endured suffering. Additionally, Job received a new family of children.

It is OK to be anxious while we are going through challenging circumstances, as the story of Job reminds us. But it's also crucial to turn to God in prayer and have faith in His power. Even though we are lost and feel alone, God will never leave us.

ACTIVITY

We may utilize prayer as a strong technique to deal with anxiety. When we pray, we are letting God into our hearts and requesting His assistance.

While some individuals find it beneficial to write down their prayers, others would rather do so in silence. Write a prayer to God in which you express your fears and anxieties.

Through this practice, you may communicate with God and confide your worries in Him in a secure setting. Spend some time reflecting about the source of your anxiety. What causes you worry? Write a prayer to God in which you communicate your worries and fears after you have a clear understanding of what is troubling you.

Write your prayer on the note below

NOTE

Praying should be a habit, I will advise you to have your own prayer journal. It helps to track your progress over time to see how you are doing. Use the template below to create yours in a notebook.

PRAYER *Journal*

Jan. 2024

1	2	3	4	5	6	7	8	9	10
11	12	13	14	15	16	17	18	19	20
21	22	23	24	25	26	27	28	29	30

OUTCOME

Todays Anxiety Prayer

I am Grateful for...

Today's Mood

PRAYER *Journal*

Feb. 2023

1	2	3	4	5	6	7	8	9	10
11	12	13	14	15	16	17	18	19	20
21	22	23	24	25	26	27	28	29	30

Todays Anxiety Prayer

OUTCOME

I am Grateful for...

Today's Mood

How do you feel about your anxiety before you pray?

_____

_____

_____

How do you feel after you pray?

_____

_____

_____

Say this prayer

Dear God,

I want to practice talking to You more, especially when I'm nervous. Please assist me to remember that You are always willing to listen.

Help me to discover the appropriate words to use and the appropriate level of peace to experience. I'm grateful that you are a source of comfort and power for me.

In Jesus's Amen.

Meditate on these Bible Verses

Mark 1:35 (NIV) - "Very early in the morning, while it was still dark, Jesus got up, left the house and went off to a solitary place, where he prayed."

Luke 18:1 (NIV) - "Then Jesus told his disciples a parable to show them that they should always pray and not give up."

Romans 12:12 (NIV) - "Be joyful in hope, patient in affliction, faithful in prayer."

CHAPTER 3

Peace in Pages

JESUS CALM THE STORM

The biblical story of Jesus calming the storm is a well-known illustration of how God's promises may ease our anxiety. When a storm developed, the disciples were aboard a boat on the Sea of Galilee.

The boat was on the verge of sinking due to the intense waves. The disciples started to scream for aid to Jesus because they were so scared.

Jesus awoke from his slumber and exclaimed, "Peace! "Be still!" The waves and wind stopped right away, and the water became quiet.

The disciples were amazed and asked Jesus, "Who is this? Even the wind and the waves obey him!"

This narrative shows us that Jesus has influence over nature, even storms. He is able to soothe our worries and bring us comfort when things are bad.

ACTIVITY

There are several assurances of peace in the Bible. In the Bible, the word "peace" is referenced more than 300 times. When we are feeling anxious, these promises might provide us solace and hope.

Trace the bible verses below to memorize a Bible Verse About Peace and use it whenever you are feeling anxious. This practice can assist you in keeping your attention on God's promises of peace and in recalling them when you are experiencing anxiety.

Create a colorful bookmark with your preferred calming Bible verse after that. Cut a bookmark shape out of a piece of cardstock or construction paper. Then, using markers or colored pencils, put your favorite, relaxing Bible quote on the bookmark. Additionally, you may adorn the bookmark with stickers or other components.

Trace the words below and memorize them

PEACE

BE

STILL

Trace the words below and memorize them

THE LORD

IS MY

SHEPHERD

I

LACK

NOTHING

Trace the words below and memorize them

FOR GOD

HAS NOT

GIVEN US

THE

SPIRIT

OF

FEAR

Practice with these bookmarks before doing yours

PEACE BE STILL

Practice with these bookmarks before doing yours

The lord is my shepherd

What Bible verse about peace speaks to you the most? Why?

_____

_____

_____

What does this verse mean to you? How can it help you to find peace in your life?

_____

_____

_____

Say this prayer

Dear God,

I'm keen on finding out how to combat my emotions of anxiety by reading your Bible verses.

Allow your promises to give me solace and courage.

Show me how to replace my anxiety with your truth. I'm grateful that you protect me from terror.

In Jesus's Amen.

Meditate on these Bible Verses

Psalm 34:4 (NIV) - "I sought the LORD, and he answered me; he delivered me from all my fears."

Matthew 6:34 (NIV) - "Therefore do not worry about tomorrow, for tomorrow will worry about itself. Each day has enough trouble of its own."

1 Peter 5:7 (NIV) - "Cast all your anxiety on him because he cares for you."

Psalm 55:22 (NIV) - "Cast your cares on the LORD and he will sustain you; he will never let the righteous be shaken."

CHAPTER 4

Peaceful You

THE STORY OF MARY MAGDALENE

Mary Magdalene was a person who struggled with depression and anxiety. She was leading a life of depravity and had been possessed by demons. But Jesus found her and gave her healing. He expelled the demons and absolved her of her sins.

For what Jesus had done for Mary Magdalene, she was incredibly appreciative. She ended up being among his most dedicated supporters. Even when others had doubts, she was always there to encourage him.

Mary Magdalene visited the tomb after Jesus had been crucified to anoint his corpse. However, when she arrived, she discovered that the tomb was empty. She learned that Jesus had resurrected from the grave from the angels.

Mary Magdalene was really happy. She sprinted to spread the good news to the other disciples. She wasn't nervous or depressed anymore. In Jesus, she had discovered serenity.

The life of Mary Magdalene serves as a reminder that God is able to help us get over our fears and feelings of sadness. God is always with us, no matter how hopeless things may appear. He is able to provide us with health and peace.

ACTIVITY

Jesus made promises to us before ascending into heaven, and it is now up to us to embrace the blessings he offered. His sacrifice on the cross has brought us peace that surpasses all concerns.

Within the clouds in the diagram below, write the names of people, situations, or things that make up the anxiety in your life.

Then, use a pale blue crayon to shade the whole cloud and write all the promises of Jesus that are stated in the box space below.

Find a quiet place, read the verses where these promises were made by Jesus, and allow it sit in your heart and you will see there's peace within you from our Christ.

JESUS'S PROMISE

Salvation and Eternal Life John 3:16 (NIV)	Rest for the Weary Matthew 11:28 (NIV)
Peace John 14:27 (NIV)	Guidance and Direction John 10:14 (NIV)
Provision and Care Matthew 6:26 (NIV)	Answered Prayer John 15:7 (NIV)
Abundant Life John 10:10 (NIV)	The Holy Spirit John 14:16 (NIV)
His Presence Always Matthew 28:20 (NIV)	Victory Over Death John 11:25 (NIV)
Love and Unity John 13:34 (NIV)	Counsel and Wisdom John 14:26 (NIV)

What did you feel covering all your worries with all the promises of Jesus?

_____

_____

_____

Which promise of Jesus Christ do you find most comforting and why?

_____

_____

_____

Say this prayer

Dear God,

I'd like to learn how to control my anxiousness using your promises. Please remind me that you are with me at all times, leading and guarding me.

Teach me to put my faith in your promises when I'm worried. I'm grateful for your love and your encouragement.

In Jesus's Amen.

Meditate on these Bible Verses

Matthew 28:20 (NIV) - "And surely I am with you always, to the very end of the age."

John 14:27 (NIV) - "Peace I leave with you; my peace I give you. I do not give to you as the world gives. Do not let your hearts be troubled and do not be afraid."

John 16:33 (NIV) - "I have told you these things, so that in me you may have peace. In this world you will have trouble. But take heart! I have overcome the world."

CHAPTER 5

The Worry Eater

Parable of the Lilies in the field

Jesus teaches his disciples not to worry by using a story about the lilies of the field in the Bible. Matthew 6:25-34 is where the narrative is located.

In the story, Jesus likens humans to lilies of the field.

He claims that despite not worrying about their food or clothing, lilies are nonetheless lovely and well-cared for. Jesus then reassures his followers that they don't need to worry either because God already knows what they require.

This parable demonstrates to us the pointlessness of worrying. Worrying about things we can't control doesn't accomplish anything.

God is aware of our needs and will meet them. Instead, we need to put our attention on believing in God and being in the here and now.

ACTIVITY

I want you to simply "Worry," in this specific activity. Write out what makes you anxious, and rank them according to the level of anxiety it causes you.

Then write out what you are most worried about in the circle below and set a timer for five (5) minutes, use this period to worry and be anxious as much as you can.

When you are done feeling anxious and worrying, write out what has changed about the situation inside the space below.

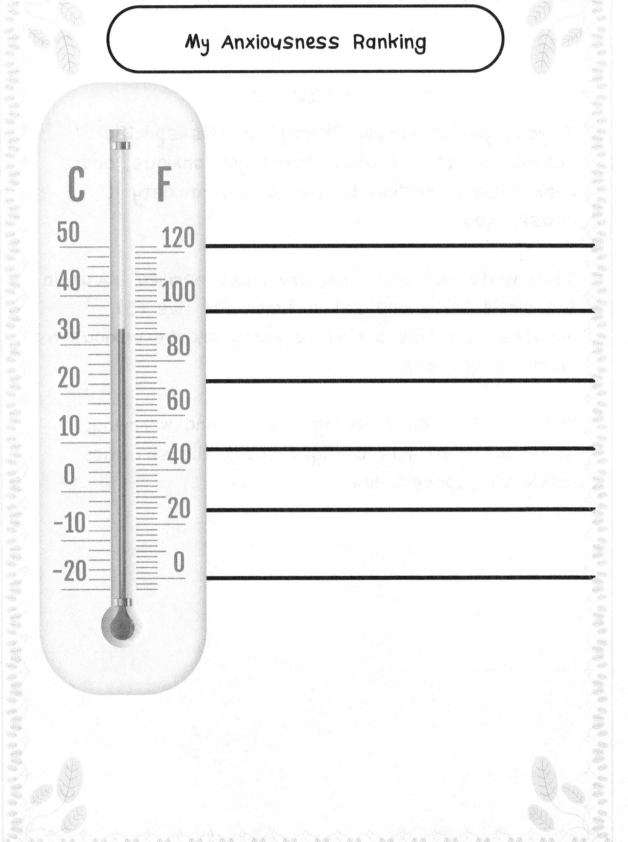

My Anxiousness Ranking

5mins

Top of my
worry list

What changed?

How does it feel to purposefully worry about something for five minutes?

_____

_____

_____

How can excessive worry affect your body and mind?

_____

_____

_____

Say this prayer

Dear God,

I want to learn how to put my faith in you and stop worrying. Please remind me that you are in charge and that you care about me.

Teach me to appreciate each day and put my troubles in your capable hands. I appreciate you being my peace.

In Jesus's Amen.

Meditate on these Bible Verses

Luke 12:25-26 (NIV) - "Who of you by worrying can add a single hour to your life? Since you cannot do this very little thing, why do you worry about the rest?"

Psalm 34:4 (NIV) - "I sought the LORD, and he answered me; he delivered me from all my fears."

Psalm 37:5 (NIV) - "Commit your way to the LORD; trust in him and he will do this."

CHAPTER 6

Positivity Jar

THE STORY OF THE WIDOW'S MITE

Jesus narrates a parable in the Bible about a widow who donates a little sum of money to the temple treasury. The narrative appears in Mark 12:41-44.

Jesus observes individuals depositing money into the temple treasury while seated there in the narrative.

He observes wealthy individuals depositing enormous sums of cash, but he also observes a destitute widow depositing two little copper pennies.

Jesus calls his disciples to him and says, "This poor widow has put in more than all the others. All these people gave their gifts out of their wealth; but she out of her poverty put in all she had to live on."

This narrative shows us the value of appreciating what we have, no matter how small it may be. Jesus valued the widow's offering more than the vast sums of money that the affluent people contributed because she sacrificed all she needed to survive.

When we are feeling nervous, the widow's mite story might help us change our viewpoint. When we're nervous, it's simple to concentrate on the things we don't have. But if we stop for a moment to be thankful for what we already have, it might make us feel happier and less stressed.

ACTIVITY

When we practice gratefulness, we pause to recognize the positive aspects of our life. This can make us feel less worried and help us perceive the world more positively.

Use the space below to write down 10 things you are grateful for and then proceed to create a "Joy Jar" to collect notes of positive moments. Every time you experience something positive, write it down on a piece of paper and put it in the jar.

You can read the messages that are in the jar if you are feeling nervous. This can aid in perspective-shifting and helping you recall the positive aspects of your life.

10 Things I'm grateful for;

Positivity Jar;

health

family

gratitude

sunshine

rainbows

education

friends

love hindsight

How can focusing on gratitude shift your perspective during anxious times?

_____

_____

_____

How can focusing on gratitude shift your perspective during anxious times?

_____

_____

_____

Say this prayer

Dear God,

To combat my anxiousness, I'd like to learn how to be appreciative. Help me in remembering your love and noticing the positive things around me.

Teach me to put my troubles aside and concentrate on the good. Thank you for all the blessings you give.

In Jesus's Amen.

Meditate on these Bible Verses

1 Thessalonians 5:18 (NIV) - "Give thanks in all circumstances, for this is God's will for you in Christ Jesus."

Psalm 107:1 (NIV) - "Give thanks to the LORD, for he is good; his love endures forever."

James 1:17 (NIV) - "Every good and perfect gift is from above, coming down from the Father of the heavenly lights, who does not change like shifting shadows."

CHAPTER 7

Imagining the worse

ISRAELITES AND THE RED SEA

According to the Bible, the Egyptians held the Israelites as slaves for a long time. God responded to their cries for assistance by sending Moses to lead them out of Egypt.

The Israelites made their way out of Egypt and toward the Promised Land. However, they were halted when they reached the Red Sea.

The Egyptians were pursuing them from behind while the sea was in front of them.

Israelites were terrified. They believed they were going to pass away. They worried that they might be caught by the Egyptians and sold into slavery once more.

But God managed to relax the Israelites. He assured them they had nothing to fear and split the Red Sea to allow them to pass. The Egyptians perished in the water while the Israelites crossed it on dry land.

The story shows us that even in the face of fear, God is present. He can assist us overcome our worries and any obstacle. Because God is with us and will look out for us, we don't need to worry about the worst-case scenario.

ACTIVITY

Draw a picture or write about anything that makes you feel really worried in each of the places provided below.

then continue by outlining what you believe the worst-case scenario is that could occur.

Next, mark the percentage that accurately represents the likelihood of this worst-case scenario occurring.

Then, explain what you would do if the worst occurred. Will you whine like the Israelites or pray to God and confront your fear like Moses?

My fear

Worse that could happen?

What will be your response?

My fear

Worse that could happen?

What will be your response?

What do you stand to gain if you face this anxiety task?

_____

_____

_____

What do you stand to gain if you don't face this anxiety task?

_____

_____

_____

Say this prayer

Dear God,

I need your assistance to understand how to deal with a difficult task that lies ahead. Please grant me fortitude and stamina.

Please remind me that you are beside me. Help me to overcome this obstacle. I appreciate you being there for me.

In Jesus's Amen.

Meditate on these Bible Verses

Psalm 34:17 (NIV) - "The righteous cry out, and the LORD hears them; he delivers them from all their troubles."

Matthew 17:20 (NIV) - "Truly I tell you, if you have faith as small as a mustard seed, you can say to this mountain, 'Move from here to there,' and it will move. Nothing will be impossible for you."

Psalm 121:1-2 (NIV) - "I lift up my eyes to the mountains-where does my help come from? My help comes from the LORD, the Maker of heaven and earth."

CHAPTER 8

Coping Skills Club

THE STORY OF JOSEPH

Joseph was a young man in the Bible who received a coat of many colors from his father. Because of their envy for Joseph, his brothers sold him into slavery. When Joseph arrived in Egypt, he was imprisoned.

Joseph employed his coping mechanisms when he was incarcerated to maintain optimism and hope.

He prayed to God in the hope that God would intervene to assist him. Additionally, he made acquaintances and developed new talents while he was incarcerated.

Joseph was eventually allowed to leave jail and given command over all of Egypt. During a period of famine, he assisted Egypt by applying his knowledge and abilities. In addition, he was able to forgive his brothers for everything they had done to him after being reunited with his family.

This anecdote shows us that we can use our coping mechanisms to get through any obstacle. We can turn to God in prayer and believe that he will aid us.

Additionally, we may use our free time to meet new people and develop new talents. Even while facing challenging circumstances, these items can support our ability to maintain optimism and hope.

ACTIVITY

Look over the list of healthy coping mechanisms that work for you. After thinking about things that make you happy, ease tension, and give you a sense of serenity, take action.

The list of coping mechanisms that will be suggested for you will only be able to minimize your anxious thoughts if you constantly use them. If you simply do it once, it's doubtful that anything will change.

You must do this as frequently as you can each day to really enjoy its benefits.

CALM FAITH BASED SONGS

Create a playlist of faith based songs;

Create Playlist
Welcome to my favorite.

▶ 04.15

▶ 04.22

▶ 03.41

▶ 04.00

▶ 04.15

▶ 04.22

▶ 03.41

▶ 04.00

▶ 04.15

⏸ ⌃

HOBBIES OR CREATIVE ACTIVITIES

Engaging in hobbies or creative activities

Painting or Drawing

Playing a musical instrument

Gardening

Crocheting or other crafting   work

Photography

Yoga or meditation

Coloring Pages for you;

pig

penguin

Write a list of the coping skills you like and why?

_____

_____

_____

How do you feel when using a coping skill?

_____

_____

_____

Say this prayer

Dear God,

To deal with my anxiety, I want to learn how to employ coping mechanisms. Help me find wholesome techniques for controlling my anxieties.

Please remind me to always keep you by my side. I appreciate your courage and solace.

In Jesus's Amen.

Meditate on these Bible Verses

Psalm 94:19 (NIV) - "When anxiety was great within me, your consolation brought me joy."

Psalm 139:23-24 (NIV) - "Search me, God, and know my heart; test me and know my anxious thoughts. See if there is any offensive way in me, and lead me in the way everlasting."

Matthew 6:34 (NIV) - "Therefore do not worry about tomorrow, for tomorrow will worry about itself. Each day has enough trouble of its own."

CHAPTER 9

Worry Pals

THE STORY OF DAVID AND JONATHAN

David and Jonathan were close friends in the Bible. They were both warriors in the army of King Saul. Jonathan was the son of the king, and David was a little shepherd kid.

David and Jonathan maintain a tight bond.

They opened up to one another about everything, even their worries and fears. David could always talk to Jonathan, and he was there to listen and give him counsel.

David was experiencing a lot of anxiety one day. He feared that King Saul would execute him. He went to Jonathan and expressed his feelings to him.

After listening to David, Jonathan assured him not to be concerned. He assured David of his safety by promising to check with his father, King Saul.

Jonathan pleaded with his father to spare David. David was quite appreciative of Jonathan's assistance. He was aware that Jonathan would always be there for him, no matter what.

The story demonstrates the value of having friends and family who are encouraging. We may feel less isolated and more supported when we have individuals we can talk to about our worry. It can also aid us in better anxiety management.

ACTIVITY

It is crucial to ask your friends and family for help if you are experiencing anxiety. They might be a really useful tool for you as you try to control your anxiety.

They could be able to help you emotionally. It might be beneficial to chat to someone who cares about you and who understands your situation when you're feeling worried. You can receive words of support and encouragement from your family and friends, which will make you feel less isolated.

Then choose one of these reliable people and talk about your worry with them. Fill the circle with names of people you can talk to about anxiety.

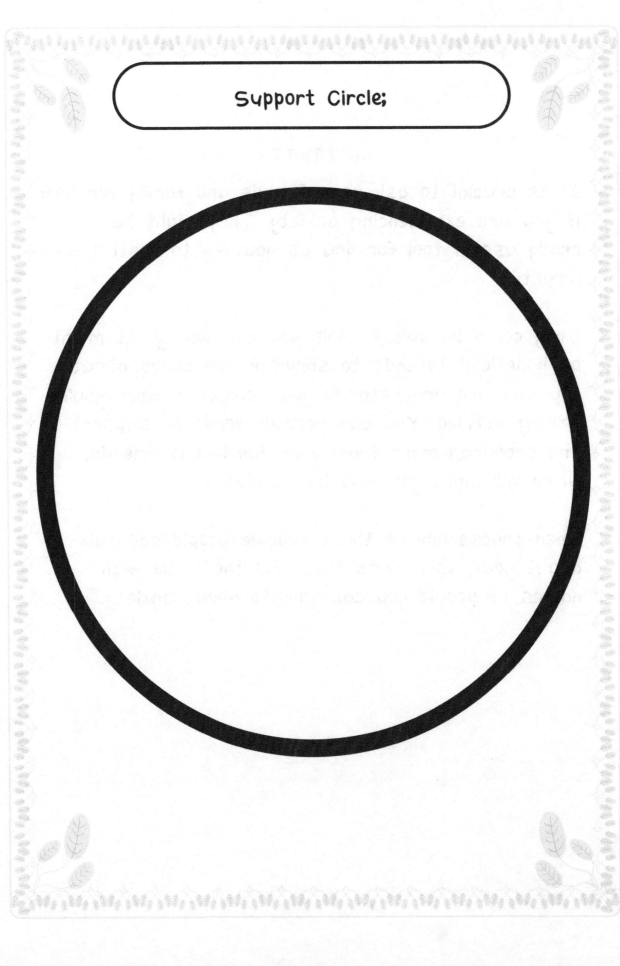

Support Circle;

How did you feel before discussing your anxiety with someone you trust?

_____

_____

_____

How did you feel after the discussion?

_____

_____

_____

Say this prayer

Dear God,

I want to learn how to talk to my family and friends about my anxiety. Please give me the confidence to confide in them.

Help them comprehend what I'm experiencing. Thank you for giving me people who care about me.

In Jesus's Amen.

Meditate on these Bible Verses

Proverbs 17:17 (NIV) - "A friend loves at all times, and a brother is born for a time of adversity."

Proverbs 12:25 (NIV) - "Anxiety weighs down the heart, but a kind word cheers it up."

Galatians 6:2 (NIV) - "Carry each other's burdens, and in this way you will fulfill the law of Christ."

CHAPTER 10

Let Go and Let God

THE STORY OF MOSES

Israelites were freed from slavery in Egypt by a Hebrew named Moses. He first resisted taking on this responsibility, but he ultimately consented and trusted God to assist him.

He aided the Israelites in getting away from Egypt and journeying across the desert by using his leadership abilities and confidence in God.

Through Moses, we learn that even in the face of insurmountable obstacles, we can rely on God to provide for us. We may succeed when we relinquish control and allow God to rule.

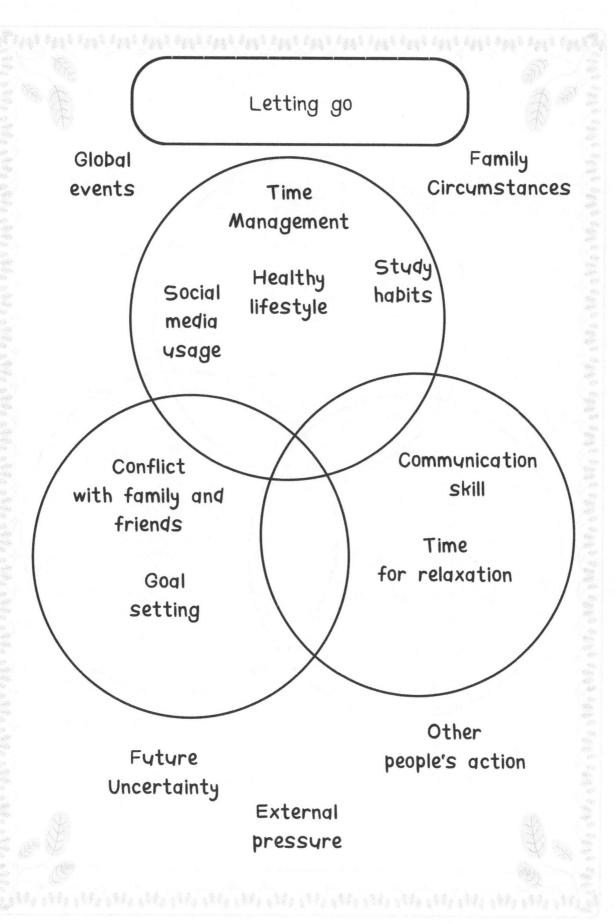

Letting go

Global events

Family Circumstances

Time Management

Social media usage

Healthy lifestyle

Study habits

Conflict with family and friends

Goal setting

Communication Skill

Time for relaxation

Future Uncertainty

External pressure

Other people's action

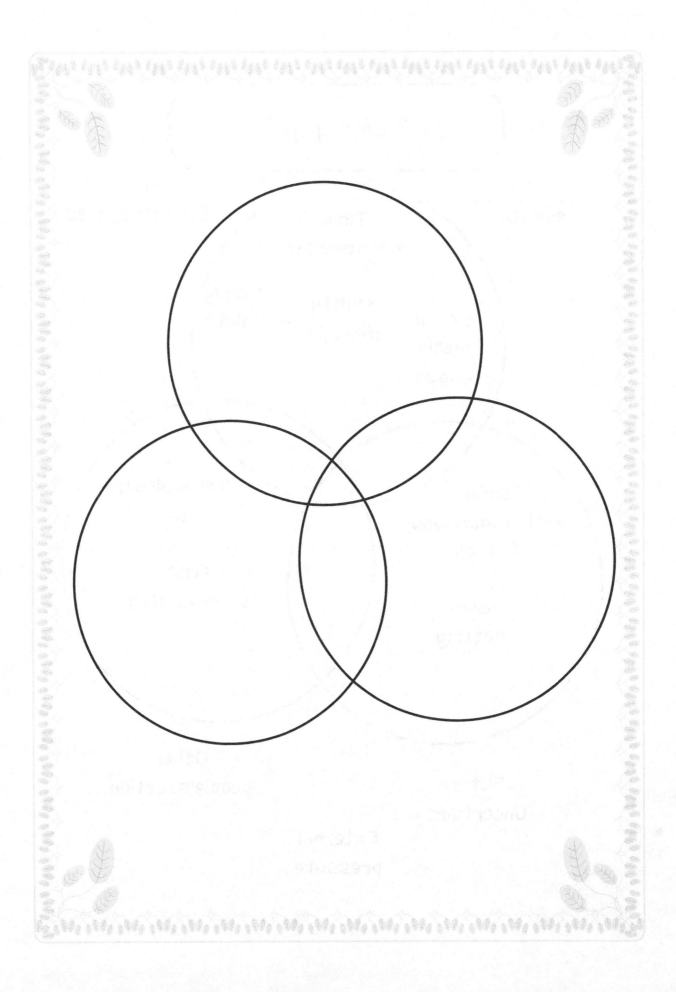

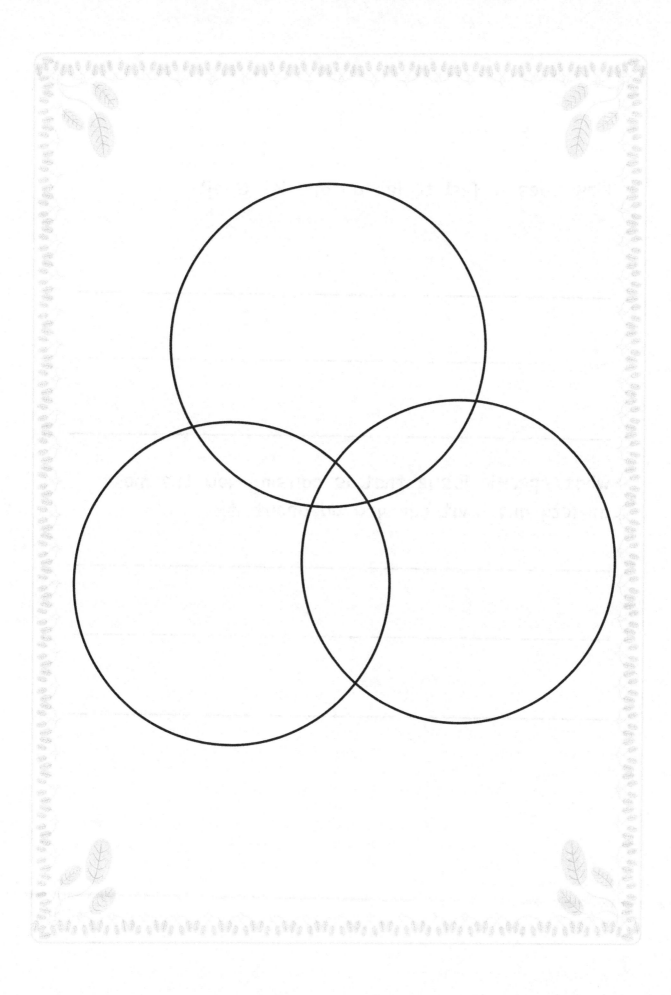

How does it feel to let go and let God?

_____

_____

_____

what specific issue that is causing you the most
anxiety and what can you do about it?

_____

_____

_____

Say this prayer

Dear God,

I want to discover how to let go of my worry and fully rely on You. Please assist me in giving You my problems.

Help me find tranquility in Your presence. I appreciate you being my safe haven.

In Jesus's Amen.

Meditate on these Bible Verses

Philippians 4:6-7 (NIV) - "Do not be anxious about anything, but in every situation, by prayer and petition, with thanksgiving, present your requests to God. And the peace of God, which transcends all understanding, will guard your hearts and your minds in Christ Jesus."

Psalm 55:22 (NIV) - "Cast your cares on the LORD and he will sustain you; he will never let the righteous be shaken."

Psalm 46:10 (NIV) - "Be still, and know that I am God; I will be exalted among the nations, I will be exalted in the earth."

Leave a Review

Be among the first set of individuals to rate this book and change the lives of others. Please do not be silent about the outcome of this book.

Lets hear from you. Thank you.

Made in the USA
Monee, IL
27 September 2024